The Lord's Prayer:
THE PRAYER JESUS TAUGHT

by Barbara Owen Webb
illustrated by James Cummins

CONCORDIA
Publishing House
St. Louis

With loving appreciation
to my children's godparents:
Anna Cooper Dyer
Betty Meissner Morse
William H. Cullember

The translation of The Lord's Prayer is from *Lutheran Worship*, copyright © 1982 by Concordia Publishing House. Used by permission.

Copyright © 1986 Concordia Publishing House
3558 S. Jefferson Avenue, St. Louis, MO 63118-3968
Manufactured in the United States of America

Library of Congress Cataloging-in-Publication Data

Webb, Barbara Owen.
    The Lord's Prayer.

    Summary: Presents one version of the Lord's prayer and explains what each line means.
    1. Lord's prayer—Juvenile literature.
[1. Lord's prayer] I. Cummins, Jim, 1914- , ill. II. Title.
BV232.W43   1986   226'.96   85-17063
ISBN 0-570-08529-2

1 2 3 4 5 6 7 8 9 10 PP 95 94 93 92 91 90 89 88 87 86

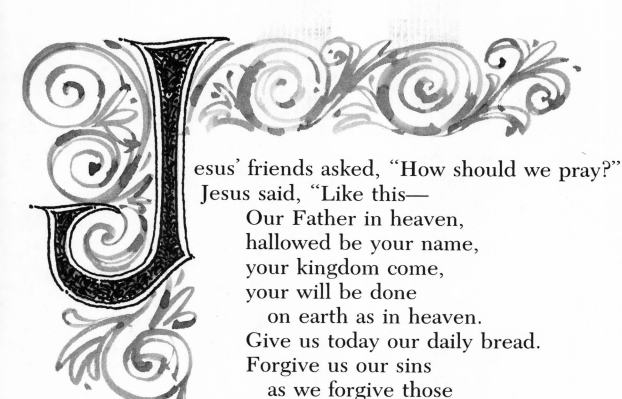

Jesus' friends asked, "How should we pray?"
Jesus said, "Like this—
Our Father in heaven,
hallowed be your name,
your kingdom come,
your will be done
    on earth as in heaven.
Give us today our daily bread.
Forgive us our sins
    as we forgive those
    who sin against us.
Lead us not into temptation,
but deliver us from evil.
For the kingdom, the power,
    and the glory are yours
    now and forever. Amen."

We can be sure God is happy to hear
the prayer Jesus taught.
Let's think about what His prayer means.

Our Father in heaven

God wants us to call Him *Father*
    just as we call a parent *Dad* or *Mom*.
Because God is our heavenly Father,
    He can do all things.
He can and will take care of us—
    you and me and all Christians.
We pray for each other and with each other
    when we say, *Our Father in heaven*.

Hallowed be your name

God's name is like a great, shining treasure
    that He gives to us.
We *hallow* it, keep it shining,
    by telling other people about Jesus
    and by doing kind deeds.

But we make this treasure look dull to others
    when we do wrong.
We ask God's help to keep His name special
    when we work and play.
We say, *Hallowed be your name.*

Your kingdom come

God's kingdom is God's special closeness to us.
It will be here at the end of time
    when we will see God and be with Him in heaven.
But God's kingdom, that special closeness,
    comes to us now when we hear His Word, the Bible.
    There the Holy Spirit tells us about our Savior, Jesus.

The Holy Spirit helps us to love God
    and to care about other people.
God's kingdom comes to more people
    when we tell others about Jesus.
We want the Holy Spirit to keep teaching us
    and others about our Savior.
So we pray, *Your kingdom come.*

Your will be done on earth as in heaven

God's will is everything He wants to do for us
    and everything He wants *us* to do for others.
He wants to help us and forgive us;
    that's why He sent Jesus to be our Savior.

Jesus helps *us* to love, to help,
and to be kind to each other.
We pray for God's love to come to all people
and for His help to do what He wants. So we pray,
Your will be done.

Give us today our daily bread

We pray with and for each other
    for all the good things we need
    to have a happy life as God's children.
Daily bread means everything
    we need, one day at a time—
    for example, food and clothes,
    family and friends, good government and peace.
God cares about *everything* we need today,
    so Jesus taught us to say, *Give us today our daily bread.*

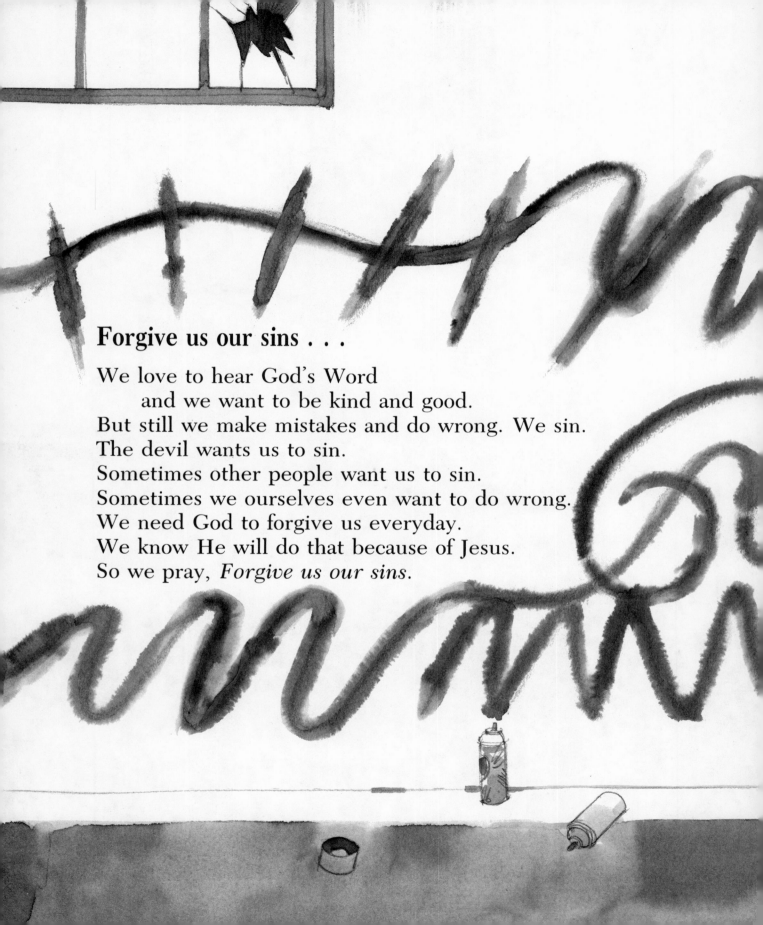

Forgive us our sins . . .

We love to hear God's Word
      and we want to be kind and good.
But still we make mistakes and do wrong. We sin.
The devil wants us to sin.
Sometimes other people want us to sin.
Sometimes we ourselves even want to do wrong.
We need God to forgive us everyday.
We know He will do that because of Jesus.
So we pray, *Forgive us our sins.*

. . . as we forgive those who sin against us.

How happy we are that God forgives us!
He doesn't even think about our sin anymore.

Since God forgives all our sins.
    we can forgive other people
    who are mean or unkind to us.
We promise God
    we will *forgive those who sin against us*.

Lead us not into temptation . . .

God protects us from temptation
    when He keeps us from doing wrong
    or getting into trouble.
Sometimes He uses other people
    to keep us out of trouble.
Sometimes He uses our conscience
    to remind us what is right and wrong.
We are glad for His help and want it every day.
    So we pray, *Lead us not into temptation.*

. . . but deliver us from evil

God wants only good for us.
But the devil wants evil or bad things—
    things like fights, swearing,
      arguing, hitting, being selfish, and forgetting God.
These are part of the devil's evil plan.

But God will help us.
> Sometimes He takes away the bad things.
> Sometimes God makes us strong against the evil.

We will finally get away from
> all bad things and unhappiness
> when we are in heaven.

We ask God to make us strong and to protect us
> when we say, *but deliver us from evil.*

For the kingdom, the power,
and the glory are yours
now and forever. Amen.

God is *King* of all.
He alone has the *power* to answer our prayers.
We give Him praise and *glory*
    for all He has done for us.
Then we say *Amen*. It means, "Yes!
    God has heard our prayer,
    and He will answer!"
AMEN!

A NOTE TO PARENTS:

Years ago almost every child learned the Lord's Prayer. Today fewer children learn the prayer by heart. Even then, they may not understand what they are praying. This book will help you share a basic understanding of this special prayer with your child.

This book is to be shared. Read the explanation together. Talk about examples from the everyday life of your child. Some words may need further explanation—*sin, conscience, will, devil, Savior, evil, love, temptation, Holy Spirit*. As you discuss these, use concrete situations along with simple, straightforward sentences. Remember: a small child cannot think in the abstract.

May our heavenly Father bless this time with your child.

Barbara Owen Webb